The Strategic Internal Marketing Guide for Transforming Your Employees

Copyright © 2024 Reginaldo Osnildo
All rights reserved.

PRESENTATION

INTRODUCTION TO STRATEGIC ENDOMARKETING

UNDERSTANDING DEMOTIVATION IN THE WORKPLACE

ESTABLISHING THE FOUNDATIONS OF ENDOMARKETING

ENDOMARKETING STRATEGY PLANNING

EFFECTIVE COMMUNICATION IN ENDOMARKETING

ORGANIZATIONAL CULTURE AND ENDOMARKETING

RECOGNITION AND VALUATION OF EMPLOYEES

TRAINING AND DEVELOPMENT THROUGH ENDOMARKETING

PROMOTING WELL-BEING IN THE WORKPLACE

CONSTRUCTIVE FEEDBACK AND OPEN DIALOGUE

CORPORATE EVENTS AND TEAM BUILDING ACTIVITIES

DIGITAL ENDOMARKETING

INCORPORATING GAMIFICATION

CORPORATE SOCIAL RESPONSIBILITY AND ENDOMARKETING

MEASURING ENDOMARKETING SUCCESS

OVERCOMING CHALLENGES IN ENDOMARKETING

ENDOMARKETING FOR DIFFERENT GENERATIONS

SUSTAINABILITY AND ENDOMARKETING

THE ART OF LISTENING IN ENDOMARKETING

ENDOMARKETING AND THE EMPLOYEE EXPERIENCE

INNOVATION AND CREATIVITY IN ENDOMARKETING

LEADERSHIP AND ENDOMARKETING

BUILDING AN ENDOMARKETING TEAM

TRANSFORMING THEORY INTO ACTION

REGINALDO OSNILDO

PRESENTATION

Welcome to the beginning of a remarkable transformation within your company. This book, **"The Strategic Internal Marketing Guide for Transforming Your Employees"**, is more than a manual; it is an invitation to embark on a journey towards organizational excellence, employee engagement and the building of a vibrant and positive work culture. You're about to discover how internal marketing, an often underappreciated approach, can be the catalyst for a workplace where every team member not only aspires to be their best, but also feels valued, motivated, and integrally part of the team. company success.

In the following pages, you will find a refined synthesis of traditional and modern knowledge about internal marketing, all presented in a practical and accessible way. This is not just a compendium of theories; is a living guide, breathing new life into established concepts and updating them for today's ever-changing world. By reading this book, you will be equipped with the tools and knowledge necessary to develop and execute an effective internal marketing program, transforming unmotivated employees into an engaged and dedicated workforce.

From the introduction to strategic internal marketing, understanding the root of demotivation in the workplace, to innovative approaches such as digital internal marketing and gamification, each chapter has been carefully designed to guide you, step by step, through the process of creating and implementing strategies effective internal marketing. This book is intended to be your companion in promoting a strong organizational culture and a positive work environment, where employee well-being is prioritized and communication is the key to success.

As we move from chapter to chapter, you will be constantly reminded that the success of any internal marketing initiative begins with understanding and applying the concepts we discuss here. Each section is designed not just to inform, but to inspire action and reflection. And at the end of each chapter, an invitation to the next stage of your journey, ensuring a continuous and engaging reading experience.

Get ready to discover how to transform your team, promote a healthier and more productive work environment, and make your company a place where everyone wants to be. "**The Strategic Internal Marketing Guide for Transforming Your Employees**" is ready to be your ally on this journey. Are you ready to get started?

Yours sincerely

Reginaldo Osnildo

INTRODUCTION TO STRATEGIC ENDOMARKETING

Endomarketing, or internal marketing, is a fundamental strategy for transforming the work environment and engaging employees in a deep and meaningful way. But, after all, what does it really mean and how important is it in building a dedicated and motivated team? In this chapter, you will discover exactly that, in addition to understanding how this approach can be the difference in transforming unmotivated employees into a vibrant and engaged workforce.

DEFINING ENDOMARKETING

Internal marketing is a practice that consists of applying marketing strategies aimed at the company's internal audience, that is, its employees. The objective is to create a positive work environment, increase engagement and satisfaction, promote an organizational culture aligned with the company's values and, consequently, improve productivity and business results. Through internal marketing, you communicate missions, visions and objectives clearly, recognize and value the efforts and achievements of employees and promote a feeling of belonging and pride in being part of the company.

THE IMPORTANCE OF ENDOMARKETING

We live in a world where the employee experience is as important as the customer experience. Motivated and engaged employees are more likely to offer quality service, drive innovation and contribute to a healthy and productive work environment. Internal marketing is the tool that makes it possible to achieve these results. It helps to:

- Strengthen internal communication, ensuring that everyone is aligned and informed about the company's events and directions.

- Promote organizational culture, reinforcing expected values and behaviors, in addition to celebrating diversity and inclusion.

- Increase employee satisfaction and well-being by offering a safe, healthy and stimulating work environment.

- Encourage personal and professional development, providing opportunities for growth and learning.

UPDATING CONCEPTS FOR TODAY

The corporate world is constantly evolving, and internal marketing practices also need to adapt. Currently, with the increase in remote work and the need for flexibility, internal marketing strategies must be inclusive and comprehensive, capable of reaching and engaging employees regardless of where they are. Technology has become a great ally, allowing virtual events, online training and the use of internal communication platforms to keep everyone connected and engaged.

WHY THIS BOOK IS ESSENTIAL FOR YOU

This guide was created with you in mind and the need to update and synthesize knowledge about internal marketing, making it accessible and practical. Here, you will not just find theories, but applicable strategies that have been adapted to the current needs and challenges of organizations. You will be able to implement an effective internal marketing program that will not only transform your employees into an engaged workforce, but also promote positive change throughout the organizational culture.

Now that you understand what internal marketing is and its crucial importance in transforming employees and promoting a positive organizational culture, it's time to dive deeper. In the next chapter, we will explore the common causes of lack of motivation in the workplace and how internal marketing can be strategically used to address them. Get ready to acquire valuable insights that will be the foundation for developing effective internal marketing strategies. Let's discover together how to rekindle the flame of motivation and engagement in your team.

UNDERSTANDING DEMOTIVATION IN THE WORKPLACE

Lack of motivation in the workplace is a complex challenge that affects not only individual productivity, but also team morale and, by extension, the success of the company as a whole. In this chapter, you will delve into the common causes of this lack of motivation and discover how internal marketing can be a powerful tool for transforming a discouraging work environment into a vibrant and motivating space.

IDENTIFYING THE ROOTS OF DEMOTIVATION

To combat demotivation, it is crucial to understand its underlying causes. Some of the most common factors include:

- **Lack of recognition and appreciation:** When employees feel that their efforts are not recognized, motivation for work can significantly decrease.

- **Ineffective communication:** Poor or insufficient communication between staff and leadership can lead to misunderstandings, conflicts and a feeling of isolation.

- **Lack of professional growth and development:** The lack of opportunities to advance or learn new skills can make employees feel stagnant.

- **Negative work environment:** A toxic organizational climate, with high levels of stress, unfair competition or lack of support, can quickly deteriorate motivation.

THE ROLE OF ENDOMARKETING IN REVERSING DEMOTIVATION

Internal marketing emerges as a strategic response to these challenges, offering solutions that aim to improve employee engagement and satisfaction. Let's explore how:

- **Promote recognition:** Through internal marketing initiatives, it is possible to create recognition programs that celebrate employees' achievements and contributions, showing that each effort is valued.

- **Improve communication:** Implementing effective internal communication channels and promoting a culture of open feedback can help build a solid bridge between the team and leadership, ensuring everyone feels heard and included.

- **Offer growth opportunities:** Professional development programs and career plans, communicated and encouraged through internal marketing, can motivate employees to become more engaged with their work, knowing that the company is investing in their future.

- **Cultivate a positive environment:** Internal marketing strategies can be used to foster a healthy organizational climate, promoting well-being, collaboration and mutual respect among team members.

TRANSFORMING THEORY INTO ACTION

Knowing the causes of demotivation is just the first step. Effectively implementing internal marketing strategies that address these issues requires careful planning and an ongoing commitment to improving the work environment. I encourage you to reflect on how these factors apply to your organization and consider innovative internal marketing approaches that can be tailored to your specific needs.

Now that you have a solid understanding of the causes of lack of motivation at work and the vital role that internal marketing can play in reversing this trend, it's time to move on to the planning phase. In the next chapter, "**ESTABLING THE FOUNDATIONS OF ENDOMARKETING**," we'll dive into the basic principles that form the backbone of any successful internal marketing strategy. Get ready to turn the insights in this chapter into concrete actions that will foster a motivating and engaging work environment.

ESTABLISHING THE FOUNDATIONS OF ENDOMARKETING

Before embarking on the journey to transform the workplace through internal marketing, it is essential to understand the pillars that support an effective internal marketing strategy. This chapter is dedicated to laying those foundations, giving you the solid foundation you need to develop a program that not only meets employees' immediate needs but also drives lasting transformation in your company's culture.

UNDERSTANDING AND ALIGNMENT OF COMPANY VALUES

The first step to any successful internal marketing strategy is to ensure that there is a clear understanding and deep alignment of the company's values among all employees. That includes:

- **Vision and mission:** Ensure that everyone in the company understands where the organization is going and the purpose that guides its actions.

- **Cultural values:** Promote and live the values that define organizational culture, encouraging behaviors that reflect these principles.

EFFECTIVE COMMUNICATION

Clear and open communication is the heart of internal marketing. Developing and maintaining communication channels that allow for the two-way flow of information is crucial. This involves:

- **Diversified channels:** Use a variety of means to ensure that the message reaches everyone, considering the particularities of the modern work environment, such as remote teams.

- **Feedback:** Encourage and facilitate continuous feedback between employees and management, using it as a tool for constant improvement.

ENGAGEMENT THROUGH RECOGNITION

Recognition is a powerful motivation tool. Developing

recognition programs that are fair, transparent and aligned with company goals can mean the difference between an apathetic team and a vibrant one. This may include:

- **Performance recognition:** Celebrate individual and team achievements in a meaningful way.

- **Valorization initiatives:** Implement practices that demonstrate to employees that their health, well-being and personal development are valued by the company.

CONTINUOUS DEVELOPMENT

Offering continuous development opportunities is essential to keep employees engaged and motivated. This covers:

- **Training and education:** Provide access to training and education programs that help employees' professional and personal growth.

- **Career plan:** Develop and clearly communicate the career paths available within the company, encouraging employees to aspire to growth.

PROMOTING WELL-BEING

The well-being of employees should be a priority in any internal marketing strategy. This involves:

- **Healthy work environment:** Create a physical and psychological environment that promotes the health and well-being of employees.

- **Well-being initiatives:** Launch programs focused on the physical, mental and emotional health of employees.

With the fundamentals of internal marketing well established, you are now prepared to start planning and implementing specific strategies that will lead to the desired transformation in your organization. In the next chapter, " **ENDOMARKETING STRATEGY PLANNING**", we will dive into the step-by-step process to create a robust internal marketing plan, aligned with the company's objectives and the needs of its employees. Get ready to transform these fundamentals into concrete actions that will revitalize your company's culture and engage your team like never before.

ENDOMARKETING STRATEGY PLANNING

After establishing the fundamentals of internal marketing, the next step is to develop a strategic plan that will guide the implementation of these initiatives within your organization. A well-designed internal marketing plan is crucial to ensure that actions are aligned with the company's objectives and meet the needs of employees, promoting a motivating and engaged work environment. This chapter offers a step-by-step guide to creating your internal marketing plan, from defining objectives to executing and evaluating strategies.

SETTING CLEAR OBJECTIVES

The first step in planning your internal marketing strategies is to establish clear and measurable objectives. Ask yourself:

- What do you want to achieve with internal marketing?

- Are you looking to improve internal communication, increase employee satisfaction, promote organizational culture, or perhaps all of the above?

Having well-defined objectives is essential to guide your actions and measure the success of your initiatives.

KNOWING YOUR AUDIENCE

Understanding who your employees are and what they value is essential for developing effective internal marketing strategies. Consider:

- The different generations present in the company and their communication preferences.

- The interests, needs and challenges faced by employees.

An effective internal marketing strategy is one that resonates with the internal audience and meets their expectations.

PREPARING THE PLAN

With the objectives defined and a clear understanding of your audience, you can start creating the plan. That includes:

- **Selection of communication channels:** Decide which channels will be used to reach employees effectively, whether through intranet, newsletters, in-person or virtual meetings, among others.

- **Content development:** Plan the type of content that will be shared, ensuring that it is relevant, engaging and aligned with the company's values.

- **Schedule:** Establish a schedule for implementing the actions, considering the best moments for each initiative.

EXECUTION

The execution of your internal marketing plan must be carefully managed to ensure that strategies are implemented as planned. Is important:

- Maintain constant and clear communication.

- Encourage employee participation, creating an environment where they feel comfortable sharing feedback and ideas.

- Monitor the progress of actions and make adjustments as necessary.

EVALUATION AND ADJUSTMENTS

After implementing internal marketing strategies, it is crucial to evaluate their results. This involves:

- Analyze whether the objectives were achieved.

- Collect feedback from employees on initiatives.

- Identify areas for improvement and make adjustments to the plan as necessary.

Continuous evaluation and the willingness to adapt strategies are fundamental to the long-term success of internal marketing in your company.

With a strategically designed and executed internal marketing plan, you are on the right path to transforming the work environment and engaging your employees. In the next chapter, "**EFFECTIVE COMMUNICATION IN ENDOMARKETING**", we will delve deeper into techniques and strategies to improve internal communication, ensuring that messages not only reach all employees, but also inspire them to engage with the company's vision. Ready to explore the secrets to effective communication that can transform your organization? Let's go ahead!

EFFECTIVE COMMUNICATION IN ENDOMARKETING

Clear, open and effective communication is the central pillar of any successful internal marketing strategy. It is through communication that the company's values, objectives and recognition are transmitted to employees, strengthening organizational culture and encouraging engagement. This chapter explores techniques and strategies for optimizing internal communication, ensuring that messages not only reach all employees, but also move them to action and participation.

IDENTIFYING THE MOST EFFECTIVE COMMUNICATION CHANNELS

The first step towards effective communication is identifying the communication channels that best adapt to the needs and preferences of your employees. This may include:

- **Intranet:** A centralized platform for sharing news, updates and recognition.

- **Internal newsletters:** To keep employees informed about important events and developments.

- **Regular meetings:** Both in-person and virtual, to encourage open discussion and feedback.

- **Corporate social media:** Platforms such as Yammer or Slack, which allow for more dynamic and interactive communication.

CREATING CONTENT THAT ENGAGES

The quality and relevance of shared content are crucial for capturing contributors' attention and encouraging them to engage. Some tips include:

- **Personalize communication:** Segment messages according to different groups within the organization to ensure relevance.

- **Be clear and concise:** Avoid unnecessary jargon and ensure messages are easy to understand.

- **Include calls to action:** Encourage employees to participate, whether by giving feedback, participating in events or contributing ideas.

PROMOTING TWO-WAY COMMUNICATION

Effective communication in internal marketing is not just about transmitting messages from management to employees, but also about listening to what they have to say. Strategies to promote two-way communication include:

- **Suggestion boxes:** Physical or digital, where employees can share ideas and feedback anonymously.

- **Opinion surveys:** To collect regular feedback on a range of issues, from job satisfaction to ideas for new internal marketing initiatives.

- **Discussion forums:** Spaces where employees can discuss ideas, share feedback and collaborate on projects.

MEASURING COMMUNICATION SUCCESS

To ensure that communication strategies are effective, it is essential to measure their impact. This can be done through:

- **Engagement analysis:** Measure the opening rate of newsletters, participation in surveys and activity on internal communication platforms.

- **Employee feedback:** Collect and analyze feedback on communication effectiveness and areas for improvement.

- **Performance indicators:** Observe whether there is a correlation between effective communication and key performance indicators, such as job satisfaction and productivity.

Now that we have explored the foundations of effective

internal communication and how it can strengthen internal marketing initiatives, it is time to look beyond and understand how this communication can contribute to building and reinforcing organizational culture. In the next chapter, "**ORGANIZATIONAL CULTURE AND ENDOMARKETING**", we will delve into the intersection between effective communication and organizational culture, exploring how internal marketing can be a powerful tool for promoting a positive culture that encourages engagement and dedication. Be ready to discover how to align your communication strategies with your company's values and objectives, transforming organizational culture.

ORGANIZATIONAL CULTURE AND ENDOMARKETING

Organizational culture is the heart of any company, directly influencing employee engagement and satisfaction. It is the set of values, beliefs, rituals and norms that shape behavior and interactions in the workplace. Internal marketing, as a bridge between management and employees, plays a crucial role in promoting and reinforcing this culture. In this chapter, we will explore how internal marketing can be effectively used to cultivate a positive organizational culture, transforming not only the work environment, but also the perception and commitment of employees.

DEFINING AND COMMUNICATING ORGANIZATIONAL CULTURE

The first step to reinforcing organizational culture through internal marketing is to clearly define the company's values and beliefs. This definition must be communicated in a consistent and attractive way to all employees, using the communication channels and strategies discussed in the previous chapter. Success stories, employee testimonials and everyday examples that reflect the company's values are powerful tools for this communication.

INTEGRATING CULTURE INTO THE COMPANY'S EVERYDAY DAY

For organizational culture to be more than a set of words on a wall or website, it needs to be lived and breathed daily. This can be achieved through:

- **Rituals and celebrations:** Create events and moments that celebrate the company's values and recognize the employees who exemplify them.

- **Decisions aligned with culture:** Ensure that all business decisions, from hiring to market strategies, reflect the company's values.

- **Leadership as a model:** Leaders and managers must be the main defenders of culture, demonstrating through their actions and decisions the values that the company values.

USING ENDOMARKETING TO REINFORCE CULTURE

Internal marketing offers a series of strategies to reinforce organizational culture, including:

- **Visual communication:** Using the company's physical and virtual space to visually reinforce culture and values, through posters, murals and digital content.

- **Training and development:** Offer training and workshops that not only develop technical skills, but also cultivate the company's values and culture.

- **Continuous feedback:** Promote an environment where feedback is valued, using it to reinforce behaviors and practices aligned with the organizational culture.

MEASURING IMPACT ON ORGANIZATIONAL CULTURE

The effectiveness of internal marketing initiatives in promoting organizational culture can be measured through:

- **Organizational climate surveys:** Periodically evaluate employees' perception of the company's culture and their alignment with it.

- **Engagement analysis:** Observe changes in employee engagement and satisfaction levels as indicators of culture strengthening.

- **Direct feedback:** Collect and analyze feedback on internal marketing initiatives and their impact on the experience of the company's values.

With a strong and positive organizational culture, reinforced by effective internal marketing strategies, your company will be well positioned to attract, retain and motivate talent. However, for these efforts to translate into tangible results, it is essential to recognize and value employees in a meaningful way. In the next chapter, "**RECOGNITION AND VALUATION OF EMPLOYEES**," we will explore strategies for creating a recognition system that not only celebrates achievements but also fuels long-term motivation and commitment. Be ready to discover how to turn appreciation into a powerful tool for boosting engagement and productivity.

RECOGNITION AND VALUATION OF EMPLOYEES

Recognition and appreciation of employees are fundamental to fostering a motivating and engaging work environment. When people feel valued, they tend to dedicate themselves more, contribute more significantly to the team and the company, and maintain a positive attitude on a daily basis. This chapter discusses how to structure and implement a recognition system that celebrates achievements, reinforces organizational culture and promotes employee commitment.

UNDERSTANDING THE IMPORTANCE OF RECOGNITION

Recognition goes beyond simple praise. It should be seen as a key part of the internal marketing strategy, contributing to:

- **Increase motivation:** Recognizing employees' efforts and achievements boosts their motivation and satisfaction at work.

- **Reinforce organizational culture:** Celebrating behaviors and results that reflect the company's values helps reinforce organizational culture.

- **Improve performance:** An environment where recognition is frequent encourages everyone to maintain a high level of performance.

EFFECTIVE RECOGNITION STRATEGIES

For recognition to be effective, it must be sincere, specific, and timely. Consider the following strategies:

- **Public recognition:** Use meetings, internal bulletins or digital platforms to publicly recognize the efforts and achievements of employees.

- **Rewards programs:** Develop programs that offer tangible rewards, such as bonuses, days off or gifts, for reaching specific goals or for exemplary behavior.

- **Personalized recognition:** Understand employees'

individual preferences to offer recognition in a way that is more meaningful to each person.

- Celebrations and events: Organize regular events to celebrate important milestones, whether related to projects, company anniversaries or other significant dates.

INCORPORATING RECOGNITION IN EVERYDAY LIFE

Recognition should not be an isolated action, but rather a continuous practice integrated into the company's daily routine:

- Create a supportive environment: Encourage employees to recognize each other's efforts, promoting a culture of mutual support and appreciation.

- Leadership by example: Leaders must lead by example, regularly recognizing the contributions of team members and demonstrating the importance of recognition.

- Continuous feedback: Align recognition with constructive feedback, ensuring employees know not only that they are valued, but also how they can continue to grow and contribute.

Measuring the Impact of Recognition

Evaluating the impact of recognition initiatives is crucial to understanding their effectiveness and making adjustments as needed. This can be done through:

- Satisfaction surveys: Conduct regular surveys to measure how recognition practices affect employee satisfaction and engagement.

- Performance analysis: Observe whether there is a correlation between recognition initiatives and improvements in individual and team performance.

- Employee feedback: Collect direct feedback on recognition programs, using suggestions to improve future initiatives.

With a well-established recognition system that celebrates achievements and values each employee, your company can reach new levels of engagement and productivity. However, recognition is just one part of a comprehensive internal marketing program. In the next chapter, "**TRAINING AND DEVELOPMENT THROUGH ENDOMARKETING**", we will explore how to use internal marketing to promote training and development opportunities, contributing to the personal and professional growth of employees. Be ready to discover how continuous learning can be a powerful motivator and how it can be integrated into your internal marketing strategies.

TRAINING AND DEVELOPMENT THROUGH ENDOMARKETING

Investing in the continuous development of employees not only increases the competence and effectiveness of the workforce, but also increases the level of satisfaction and engagement. An effective training and development program, promoted through internal marketing strategies, can be a big difference in retaining talent and strengthening organizational culture. In this chapter, we will explore how to integrate training and development into your internal marketing strategies, transforming continuous learning into a pillar of motivation and growth within the company.

THE IMPORTANCE OF CONTINUOUS DEVELOPMENT

The continuous development of employees is essential for:

- **Maintain competitiveness:** Ensure that the team is always up to date with the latest trends and technologies in the sector.

- **Increase talent retention:** Offering paths for professional growth contributes to employee satisfaction and loyalty.

- **Promote innovation:** Well-trained and motivated employees are more likely to contribute innovative ideas that can move the company forward.

ENDOMARKETING STRATEGIES TO PROMOTE DEVELOPMENT

Integrating training and development into internal marketing strategies involves creating a culture that values and promotes continuous learning:

- **Communication of opportunities:** Use all available internal communication channels to publicize training opportunities, workshops and courses, highlighting how they contribute to personal and professional growth.

- **Celebrate learning achievements:** Publicly recognize and celebrate learning achievements, such as completing courses or certifications, reinforcing the importance of continuous development.

- **Incorporate development into career plans:** Clearly show how training and development fit into career plans within the company, encouraging employees to engage in their own progression.

CREATING ATTRACTIVE TRAINING PROGRAMS

For training and development programs to be effective, they must be attractive and accessible to employees:

- **Diversify learning methods:** Offer a variety of formats, such as e- learning , in-person workshops and mentoring, to suit different learning styles.

- **Involve employees in program development:** Request feedback on learning interests and desired areas of development, ensuring programs are relevant and engaging.

- **Promote peer learning:** Encourage the exchange of knowledge between colleagues by facilitating knowledge sharing sessions and study groups.

MEASURING SUCCESS AND IMPACT

Assessing the impact of training and development programs is crucial to understanding their effectiveness and making adjustments as needed:

- **Participant feedback:** Collect immediate feedback from employees after participating in training programs to assess satisfaction and applicability of learning.

- **Performance assessment:** Monitor the application of knowledge acquired at work and its impact on individual and team performance.

- **Engagement indicators:** Observe whether there is a correlation between participation in development programs and employee engagement and satisfaction levels.

Integrating training and development into your internal marketing strategies not only empowers your employees, but also contributes significantly to engagement and motivation. In the next chapter, "**PROMOTING WELL-BEING IN THE WORKPLACE**", we will explore how internal marketing initiatives can be used to support the physical, mental and emotional well-being of employees, creating a work environment where everyone can thrive. Be ready to discover how health and well-being are critical to long-term productivity and success.

PROMOTING WELL-BEING IN THE WORKPLACE

Promoting well-being in the workplace goes beyond simple benefits; it's about creating an environment where each employee feels supported in all aspects of their life, not just their professional sphere. Through internal marketing, it is possible to implement initiatives that promote physical, mental and emotional well-being, contributing to the creation of a healthy and productive work environment. In this chapter, we'll explore how these initiatives not only benefit individual employees, but also reinforce the company's commitment to comprehensive care for its team.

THE IMPORTANCE OF WELL-BEING AT WORK

Employee well-being directly impacts productivity, creativity and engagement. Work environments that promote well-being tend to have lower rates of absenteeism, turnover and internal conflicts, as well as greater job satisfaction. Therefore, investing in well-being is investing in the sustainable success of the organization.

ENDOMARKETING STRATEGIES FOR WELL-BEING

Implementing well-being initiatives requires careful planning and strategic execution, aspects in which internal marketing plays a fundamental role:

- **Communication of well-being programs:** Use internal marketing channels to inform about available health and well-being programs, such as workplace gymnastics, consultations with psychologists, nutritionists, and other preventive health initiatives.

- **Awareness campaigns:** Promote regular campaigns on important topics such as mental health, healthy eating, the importance of physical activity and relaxation and mindfulness techniques.

- **Wellness challenges:** Encourage participation in activities and challenges that promote healthy habits, such as friendly daily step competitions, reading marathons or healthy eating challenges.

CREATING A HEALTHY WORK ENVIRONMENT

In addition to specific initiatives, the physical environment and company culture play a crucial role in employee well-being:

- **Rest spaces:** Create areas where employees can relax and briefly disconnect from work, such as break rooms, green areas or meditation spaces.

- **Schedule flexibility and remote work:** Offer flexibility options that allow employees to better balance their professional and personal lives, recognizing and respecting each person's individual needs.

- **Supportive culture:** Foster a culture that values well-being, encouraging managers to be proactive in supporting the mental and physical health of their teams and promoting open dialogue about these issues.

MEASURING THE IMPACT OF WELLBEING INITIATIVES

To ensure the effectiveness of well-being initiatives, it is essential to measure their impact:

- **Satisfaction and well-being surveys:** Conduct regular surveys to assess employee perception of well-being initiatives and identify areas for improvement.

- **Absenteeism and productivity analysis:** Monitor absenteeism rates and productivity indicators before and after implementing initiatives to assess their direct impact.

- **Continuous feedback:** Encourage constant feedback on wellness programs, allowing for continuous adjustments and improvements based on employee needs.

Promoting well-being in the workplace is an ongoing journey that requires constant commitment and innovation. In the next chapter, "**CONSTRUCTIVE FEEDBACK AND OPEN DIALOGUE**", we will explore how to create an environment where feedback is not only encouraged, but used as a strategic tool for ongoing development and strengthening relationships within the team. Get ready to learn how to turn feedback into a positive force that drives personal growth, engagement, and collaboration.

CONSTRUCTIVE FEEDBACK AND OPEN DIALOGUE

Creating a work environment where constructive feedback and open dialogue are valued is essential for the continuous development of employees and strengthening relationships within the team. This chapter explores how to use internal marketing to effectively encourage and facilitate the exchange of feedback, turning it into a powerful tool for growth and improvement for everyone in the organization.

THE IMPORTANCE OF CONSTRUCTIVE FEEDBACK

Constructive feedback is essential for:

- **Promote personal and professional development:** Helps employees understand their strengths and areas for improvement.

- **Improve communication and teamwork:** Strengthens working relationships by promoting open communication and mutual trust.

- **Increase motivation and engagement:** When employees see that their opinions are valued and that they have opportunities for growth, their engagement and motivation increase.

ENDOMARKETING STRATEGIES TO PROMOTE FEEDBACK

Using internal marketing strategies to promote a culture of constructive feedback involves several actions:

- **Awareness campaigns:** Run internal campaigns that highlight the importance of constructive feedback, sharing tips on how to give and receive feedback effectively.

- **Trainings and workshops:** Offer training sessions on communication skills, including how to articulate constructive feedback and how to react positively when receiving it.

- **Digital tools:** Implement platforms that facilitate the exchange of feedback, such as internal applications where employees can give and receive feedback anonymously or not.

FOSTERING AN OPEN DIALOGUE

In addition to feedback, open dialogue between employees, teams and leaders is crucial for conflict resolution, innovation and decision making. Some ways to promote it include:

- **Regular feedback meetings:** Establish periodic meetings dedicated exclusively to exchanging feedback between team members and between employees and managers.

- **Suggestion boxes:** Maintain physical or digital suggestion boxes where employees can express their ideas, concerns and suggestions anonymously.

- **Discussion forums:** Create spaces, physical or virtual, where employees can openly discuss ideas, projects and challenges faced by the team or the company.

MEASURING THE IMPACT OF FEEDBACK AND DIALOGUE

Assessing the impact of feedback and open dialogue initiatives is vital to understanding their effectiveness:

- **Organizational climate surveys:** Use surveys to measure employees' perception of the effectiveness of feedback and openness to dialogue within the organization.

- **Performance analysis:** Observe whether there are improvements in individual and team performance correlated with the implementation of effective feedback practices.

- **Feedback on feedback:** Encourage employees to evaluate the quality and usefulness of the feedback received, as well as opening the environment for dialogue.

With an environment that values constructive feedback and

open dialogue, your organization will be well positioned to face challenges, cultivate innovation and strengthen employee engagement. In the next chapter, "**CORPORATE EVENTS AND TEAM-BUILDING ACTIVITIES**," we'll explore how onboarding activities can complement feedback initiatives, further promoting team cohesion and collaborative culture. Be prepared to discover creative strategies to unite your team and strengthen internal bonds, transforming the work environment.

CORPORATE EVENTS AND TEAM BUILDING ACTIVITIES

Corporate events and team building activities are essential for strengthening bonds between employees, promoting team cohesion and improving communication and collaboration within the company. By integrating these activities into internal marketing strategies, you can not only improve the work environment, but also reinforce organizational culture, increase employee engagement and encourage the development of interpersonal skills. This chapter focuses on how to plan and execute these events effectively, ensuring they bring tangible benefits to everyone involved.

THE VALUE OF CORPORATE EVENTS AND TEAM BUILDING

These activities offer a unique opportunity to:

- **Break the routine:** Provide employees with a break from their daily routine, helping to recharge their energy and increase productivity.

- **Improve communication:** Promote dialogue and mutual understanding, essential for the team's success.

- **Foster team spirit:** Stimulate collaboration and reinforce the idea that everyone is working towards a common goal.

- **Identify potential leaders:** Observe how employees behave in different situations, which can reveal leadership skills and other competencies.

PLANNING EFFECTIVE EVENTS AND ACTIVITIES

For team building events and activities to be successful, it is important to:

- **Set clear goals:** Determine what you hope to achieve from the event or activity, whether it's improving communication, resolving conflicts, or simply relaxing and having fun.

- **Choose appropriate activities:** Activities must be chosen based on the objectives, company culture and characteristics of the participants. Consider a variety that suits different interests and abilities.

- **Include everyone:** Ensure that activities are accessible and inclusive, allowing all employees to participate and contribute.

EXAMPLES OF TEAM BUILDING ACTIVITIES

- **Creative workshops:** Activities such as art, cooking or creative writing workshops can help stimulate creativity and offer a new perspective on co-workers.

- **Sports and team games:** Friendly competitions or team sports, such as football, volleyball or treasure hunts, promote collaboration and team spirit.

- **Corporate retreats:** A retreat outside of the work environment can be an excellent opportunity for employees to disconnect from their routine, connect on a more personal level and discuss company goals and strategies in a relaxed environment.

MEASURING SUCCESS

To evaluate the effectiveness of team-building events and activities:

- **Request feedback:** After the event, ask employees to share their impressions, what they liked most, what could be improved and suggestions for future activities.

- **Watch for changes:** Keep an eye out for changes in the workplace after the event, such as improvements in communication, increased collaboration, or more team initiatives.

- **Analyze performance impact:** Check for improvements in team performance or project completion after team building activities.

With the successful implementation of corporate events and team building activities, your organization will be on the right path to developing a more cohesive, communicative and engaged team. In the next chapter, "**DIGITAL ENDOMARKETING**", we will explore how digital tools and platforms can be used to enhance internal marketing strategies, allowing for more effective communication and continuous employee engagement. Be ready to discover how technology can be a powerful ally in promoting well-being and building a strong organizational culture.

DIGITAL ENDOMARKETING

Digital transformation has reshaped the way companies communicate internally and promote employee engagement. Digital internal marketing leverages digital tools and platforms to reach and engage your workforce more effectively, regardless of where they are. In this chapter, we explore how to integrate digital internal marketing into internal communication strategies, maximizing the reach and effectiveness of internal marketing initiatives.

THE RISE OF DIGITAL ENDOMARKETING

Digital internal marketing is not just a trend, but a necessary evolution in the face of changes in the work environment, including the growing adoption of remote work and the need for instant communication. He offers:

- **Greater reach:** Ability to reach employees in different locations, including those working remotely or in distant branches.

- **Interactivity:** Digital tools allow two-way communication, encouraging feedback and participation from employees.

- **Personalization:** Possibility of personalizing communication according to the interests and needs of specific groups of employees.

DIGITAL ENDOMARKETING TOOLS

Several tools can be used to implement digital internal marketing strategies, including:

- **Corporate intranets and portals:** Central platforms for sharing news, updates and important information with the entire team.

- **Corporate social networks:** Platforms such as Slack, Microsoft Teams or Yammer facilitate real-time communication and collaboration.

- **Mobile apps:** Customized apps for your business can provide easy access to important features, notifications, and updates.

- **Webinars and online training:** Use of online learning platforms to promote the continuous development of employees.

EFFECTIVE DIGITAL ENDOMARKETING STRATEGIES

To maximize the impact of digital internal marketing, consider the following strategies:

- **Engaging content:** Produce relevant and attractive content, such as videos, podcasts and articles that reflect the company's culture and values.

- **Interactive campaigns:** Launch campaigns that encourage active participation from employees, such as contests, polls and challenges.

- **Segmented communication:** Take advantage of digital tools to segment communication, ensuring that messages are relevant to different groups within the company.

- **Digital feedback:** Use digital platforms to collect feedback from employees, allowing for faster analysis and immediate action on suggestions and concerns.

MEASURING THE IMPACT OF DIGITAL ENDOMARKETING

The effectiveness of digital internal marketing can be assessed through:

- **Data analysis:** Digital tools offer vast amounts of data that can be analyzed to understand employee engagement and preferences.

- **Surveys and feedback:** Conduct regular digital surveys to measure satisfaction and collect feedback on digital internal marketing initiatives.

- Performance indicators: Monitor key indicators such as click-through rates, attendance at online events, and use of corporate applications to assess engagement.

By integrating digital internal marketing into your internal communication strategies, your company can create a more dynamic, inclusive and engaged work environment. In the next chapter, "**INCORPORATING GAMIFICATION**", we will explore how gamification can be used within internal marketing strategies to further increase engagement, promoting a fun and motivating work environment. Get ready to discover how games and challenges can transform the employee experience and boost productivity.

INCORPORATING GAMIFICATION

Gamification uses game elements in the non-playful context of the workplace to increase employee engagement and motivation, encouraging positive behaviors through rewards and recognition. This chapter explores how gamification can be integrated into internal marketing strategies, transforming everyday tasks into more engaging and fun experiences, while promoting learning, collaboration and healthy competition.

UNDERSTANDING GAMIFICATION

Gamification does not mean turning work into a game, but rather applying game mechanics – such as points, levels, badges, leaderboards, and missions – to improve motivation and engagement. It is based on the psychology that motivates people to achieve their goals by offering immediate recognition and rewards for specific achievements.

BENEFITS OF GAMIFICATION

- **Increased engagement:** Making tasks more fun and challenging can significantly increase employee engagement.

- **Reinforcement of learning:** Educational games and simulations can facilitate training and professional development in a more interactive and memorable way.

- **Promoting collaboration:** Gamified activities that encourage teamwork can improve communication and collaboration between employees.

- **Recognition and motivation:** Gamification provides immediate feedback through rewards and recognition, encouraging continued good performance.

GAMIFICATION IMPLEMENTATION STRATEGIES

To effectively incorporate gamification into your internal marketing initiatives, consider the following strategies:

- **Define clear objectives:** Before implementing gamification elements, it is crucial to define clear objectives. Ask yourself what you hope to achieve: Increased engagement? Improved learning and development? Greater collaboration?

- **Choose the appropriate mechanics:** Depending on the objectives, different game mechanics can be applied. For example, to promote learning, quizzes can be a great option; To encourage productivity, consider challenges with rewards.

- **Personalize the experience:** Gamification must be relevant to employees. Consider customizing activities to reflect company culture and meet team preferences.

- **Provide feedback and recognition:** Ensure that the gamification system offers constant feedback and recognizes employees' efforts and achievements in a visible and meaningful way.

MEASURING GAMIFICATION SUCCESS

Assessing the impact of gamification initiatives is essential to ensure they are meeting their objectives:

- **Employee feedback: Collecting direct feedback is vital to understand how** gamified activities are being received and what their impact is on engagement and motivation.

- **Data analysis:** Use data and analytics to measure engagement in gamified activities, observing metrics such as participation, task completion and learning progress.

- **Performance assessment:** Observe whether there is a correlation between the introduction of gamification and improvements in overall performance, including productivity, work quality and collaboration.

With gamification, you can create a more dynamic and engaging work environment, encouraging productivity, continuous learning and collaboration. In the next chapter, "**CORPORATE SOCIAL RESPONSIBILITY AND ENDOMARKETING**", we will explore how to integrate social responsibility initiatives into internal marketing strategies, promoting not only internal engagement, but also contributing positively to the community and the environment. Get ready to discover how to align company values with meaningful social actions that resonate with employees and reinforce the brand image.

CORPORATE SOCIAL RESPONSIBILITY AND ENDOMARKETING

Integrating corporate social responsibility (CSR) into internal marketing strategies not only reinforces the company's commitment to social, environmental and ethical issues, but also promotes a sense of purpose and belonging among employees. This chapter discusses how to use internal marketing to involve employees in CSR initiatives, creating a corporate culture that values positive contributions to society and the environment.

THE IMPORTANCE OF CSR IN THE CORPORATE ENVIRONMENT

CSR benefits society and the environment, but also brings significant benefits to the company, including:

- **Improved brand image:** Participation in social projects strengthens the company's image among consumers, partners and the local community.

- **Increased employee engagement:** Working for a greater cause can increase motivation and job satisfaction.

- **Talent attraction and retention:** Companies with strong CSR programs are more attractive to professionals looking for employers with values aligned with theirs.

ENDOMARKETING STRATEGIES TO PROMOTE CSR

To effectively integrate CSR into your internal marketing strategies, consider:

- **Clear communication of CSR projects:** Use internal channels to inform and update employees about CSR initiatives, highlighting their impact and how they can participate.

- **Corporate volunteering:** Organize and promote volunteer programs, encouraging the active participation of employees in social, environmental or charitable projects.

- **Awareness campaigns:** Create internal marketing campaigns that educate and raise awareness among employees about social and environmental issues, showing how their actions can make a difference.

ENGAGING EMPLOYEES IN CSR INITIATIVES

To maximize employee engagement in CSR initiatives:

- **Offer participation options:** Give employees the option to choose between different CSR projects, increasing the chances of personal involvement and commitment.

- **Recognize and reward involvement:** Celebrate employees' contributions to CSR projects, whether through internal recognition, awards or additional benefits.

- **Promote team participation:** Encourage the creation of teams to participate in CSR projects, strengthening team spirit and improving collaboration.

MEASURING THE IMPACT OF CSR INITIATIVES

Assessing the impact of CSR initiatives is crucial to understanding their effectiveness and making adjustments as needed:

- **Engagement surveys:** Conduct surveys to measure the impact of CSR initiatives on employee engagement and satisfaction.

- **Community contribution analysis:** Evaluate the impact of CSR initiatives on the community and the environment, using specific metrics whenever possible.

- **Employee feedback:** Collect direct feedback on CSR initiatives, seeking to understand what works well and what can be improved.

By integrating corporate social responsibility into your internal marketing strategies, you not only benefit the community and the environment, but also strengthen corporate culture, increase employee engagement and improve the company's image. In the next chapter, **"MEASURING ENDOMARKETING SUCCESS,"** we will explore methods and metrics for evaluating the effectiveness of your internal marketing strategies, ensuring you can adjust and improve your initiatives based on hard data. Be ready to learn how to measure the impact of your internal marketing program and use this information to drive your company's ongoing success.

MEASURING ENDOMARKETING SUCCESS

Evaluating the effectiveness of internal marketing strategies is crucial to ensure that they are achieving the desired objectives, such as increasing employee engagement, improving internal communication and strengthening corporate culture. This chapter presents methods and metrics to measure the success of your internal marketing initiatives, allowing you to adjust and improve your actions based on concrete insights.

ESTABLISHING SUCCESS METRICS

Before measuring the success of your internal marketing strategies, it is important to define which metrics will be used. Some common metrics include:

- **Employee engagement:** Measured through satisfaction surveys, participation rate in events and initiatives, and use of internal communication platforms.

- **Organizational climate:** Assessed through surveys that measure employees' perception of the work environment, corporate culture and their general well-being.

- **Employee retention and turnover:** Monitoring retention and turnover rates to assess whether internal marketing strategies are contributing to talent retention.

- **Productivity:** Analysis of performance indicators before and after the implementation of internal marketing initiatives to verify improvements in productivity.

COLLECTING AND ANALYZING DATA

For an effective analysis, consider the following steps:

- **Regular surveys:** Conduct engagement and organizational climate surveys regularly to monitor changes in employee perception.

- **Continuous feedback:** Encourage continuous feedback on internal marketing initiatives, using digital platforms that facilitate this communication.

- **Data analysis from digital platforms:** Use analytical tools from internal digital platforms to measure employee interaction and engagement.

ADJUSTING FEEDBACK-BASED STRATEGIES

With the data collected, it is possible:

- **Identify areas for improvement:** Use feedback to identify which aspects of your internal marketing initiatives need to be improved or adjusted.

- **Innovate and experiment:** Based on analysis, try new approaches and strategies to increase employee engagement and satisfaction.

- **Recognize success:** Celebrate and share the successes achieved through internal marketing initiatives, reinforcing the value of these strategies for the company and employees.

CREATING A CONTINUOUS CYCLE OF IMPROVEMENT

The measurement and adjustment process must be continuous, creating a feedback cycle that allows for constant improvement of internal marketing strategies. This involves:

- **Regular review of metrics:** Periodically reevaluate success metrics to ensure they continue to align with company objectives.

- **Adaptation to changes:** Be ready to adapt your strategies as the needs of the company and employees evolve.

- **Investment in technology:** Use emerging technologies to collect and analyze data more efficiently, facilitating the implementation of improvements.

Measuring the success of internal marketing initiatives is just the beginning. In the next chapter, "**OVERCOMING CHALLENGES**

IN ENDOMARKETING", we will cover common obstacles when implementing internal marketing programs and how to overcome them. Be prepared to learn strategies to face and overcome these challenges, ensuring that your internal marketing program not only survives, but thrives, contributing significantly to your company's success.

OVERCOMING CHALLENGES IN ENDOMARKETING

Implementing an effective internal marketing program can present several challenges, from internal resistance to the difficulty in measuring the ROI (Return on Investment) of initiatives. This chapter addresses common obstacles encountered when developing internal marketing strategies and provides practical guidance for overcoming them, ensuring that your program not only achieves its objectives, but also adds significant value to organizational culture and employee engagement.

IDENTIFYING COMMON CHALLENGES

Some of the most common challenges include:

- **Resistance to change:** Natural in any organization, resistance can come from both leadership and employees.

- **Ineffective communication:** Difficulties in reaching all employees or in transmitting messages effectively.

- **Limited budget:** Financial constraints may limit the implementation of certain initiatives.

- **Measuring results:** Challenges in establishing clear and measurable metrics to evaluate the success of internal marketing actions.

STRATEGIES TO OVERCOME CHALLENGES

For each challenge, there are potential strategies to overcome it:

- **Leadership involvement:** Obtain the support of senior leadership by demonstrating how internal marketing can align with the company's strategic objectives and contribute to its success.

- **Clear and multichannel communication:** Use different communication channels to ensure that internal marketing messages reach all employees, adapting the format and language according to the target audience.

- **Budget creativity:** Explore creative, low-cost solutions, such as virtual events or recognition programs that do not require large financial investments.

- **Definition of success metrics:** Establish clear indicators from the beginning, allowing accurate assessment of the impact of internal marketing initiatives.

SUCCESS STORIES AND LESSONS LEARNED

Learning from success stories inside and outside your industry can offer valuable insights:

- **Study success stories:** Look for examples of companies that overcame similar challenges and analyze the strategies they adopted.

- **Adaptation and flexibility:** Be open to adapting strategies based on what has worked (or not) in other contexts.

- **Collaboration and feedback:** Encourage a culture of continuous feedback, where employees can express their ideas and concerns, contributing to the continuous improvement of initiatives.

MAINTAINING LONG-TERM COMMITMENT

Overcoming challenges in internal marketing requires a continuous commitment to the evolution and adaptation of strategies:

- **Monitoring and adjustment:** Keep the feedback loop active, adjusting strategies as needed to ensure they remain relevant and effective.

- **Commitment to organizational culture:** Integrate internal marketing deeply into the company's culture, ensuring that it is perceived as an essential part of the work environment.

- **Constant innovation:** Stay up to date with new trends

in internal marketing, exploring new technologies and methodologies to keep the program fresh and engaging.

Overcoming internal marketing challenges is crucial to developing a program that not only meets the organization's current needs, but is also prepared for future demands. In the next chapter, "**ENDOMARKETING FOR DIFFERENT GENERATIONS**", we will explore how to adapt internal marketing strategies to meet the expectations and needs of a diverse workforce, ensuring that engagement initiatives are inclusive and effective for all employees, regardless of generation. that they belong.

ENDOMARKETING FOR DIFFERENT GENERATIONS

In an increasingly diverse work environment, with several generations working side by side, from baby boomers to generation Z, adapting internal marketing strategies to meet the needs and expectations of each group becomes a crucial challenge. This chapter explores how to customize internal marketing initiatives to create an inclusive environment that respects and values generational diversity, promoting engagement and collaboration among all employees.

UNDERSTANDING GENERATIONAL DIFFERENCES

Each generation brings its own experiences, expectations and preferences to the workplace:

- **Baby boomers:** Value recognition of experience and loyalty to the company. They prefer direct and personal communication.

- **Generation X:** They are independent, value work-life balance and prefer direct and constructive feedback.

- **Generation Y (Millennials):** They seek purpose at work, value continuous feedback and development opportunities. They prefer digital, but meaningful communication.

- **Generation Z:** Highly digital, they value flexibility, inclusion and are motivated by missions and social impact. They prefer quick communication across multiple digital channels.

ADAPTED ENDOMARKETING STRATEGIES

To effectively engage all generations, consider:

- **Multichannel communication:** Use a variety of channels, from in-person meetings and phone calls to digital platforms and social media, to ensure messages reach everyone effectively.

- **Personalized recognition programs:** Develop recognition systems that allow personalization, recognizing employees in a way that is more meaningful to each person, based on their generations and individual preferences.

- **Flexible development opportunities:** Offer a range of options for professional and personal development, from formal training to online learning, mentoring and innovation projects.

- **Well-being and work-life balance initiatives:** Implement programs that meet diverse well-being and work-life balance needs, recognizing that these can vary significantly between different generations.

PROMOTING INTERGENERATIONAL COLLABORATION

Encouraging the exchange of knowledge and experiences between generations can enrich the work environment and promote a culture of mutual learning:

- **Diverse work groups:** Promote the formation of teams made up of members from different generations for specific projects, encouraging collaboration and the exchange of perspectives.

- **Cross mentoring programs:** Establish mentoring programs where employees from different generations can both teach and learn, recognizing the unique value that each one brings to the company.

- **Inclusive events and activities:** Host events that are appealing to all generations, from workshops to team-building and volunteering activities.

MEASURING SUCCESS AND ADJUSTING STRATEGIES

- **Surveys and feedback:** Conduct regular surveys to understand how different generations perceive internal marketing initiatives and collect feedback for continuous adjustments.

- **Engagement analysis:** Monitor engagement by age group to assess the impact of adapted strategies and identify opportunities for improvement.

Adjusting internal marketing strategies to suit different generations is essential to creating a harmonious and productive work environment. In the next chapter, "**SUSTAINABILITY AND ENDOMARKETING**", we will explore how sustainability initiatives can be integrated into internal marketing, aligning company values with the growing demand for ecological practices and social responsibility, and how this can serve to further engage employees in all generations.

SUSTAINABILITY AND ENDOMARKETING

Integrating sustainability into internal marketing strategies not only responds to the growing demand for environmental and social responsibility, but also engages employees in a common purpose that transcends the company's purely commercial objectives. This chapter discusses how to align internal marketing initiatives with sustainable practices, promoting a corporate culture that values positive contributions to the planet and society.

THE RELEVANCE OF SUSTAINABILITY IN THE CORPORATE ENVIRONMENT

Sustainability practices can reinforce the company's image, improve employee satisfaction and attract new talent, especially those who value environmental and social responsibility. Additionally, sustainable companies often experience improved operational efficiency and long-term cost savings.

ENDOMARKETING STRATEGIES TO PROMOTE SUSTAINABILITY

To effectively integrate sustainability into your internal marketing strategies, consider the following approaches:

- **Communication of sustainable policies and practices:** Use internal channels to inform employees about the company's sustainability policies, including objectives, practices adopted and progress achieved.

- **Encouraging participation in sustainable initiatives:** Promote and facilitate employee involvement in sustainability programs, such as recycling, waste reduction, and environmental volunteering projects.

- **Training and education:** Offer training and workshops on sustainable practices, highlighting how each employee can contribute to sustainability goals at work and at home.

ENGAGING EMPLOYEES IN SUSTAINABLE PRACTICES

To maximize employee engagement in sustainability initiatives:

- **Challenges and competitions:** Organize sustainability challenges, encouraging employees to adopt greener practices and rewarding the most significant contributions.

- **Public recognition:** Celebrate sustainability actions and projects led by employees, recognizing their effort and dedication in internal communications and events.

- **Creating sustainability ambassadors:** Form a group of sustainability ambassadors within the company to lead by example and inspire other employees to get involved.

MEASURING THE IMPACT OF SUSTAINABILITY INITIATIVES

Measure the success of your sustainability initiatives through:

- **Engagement surveys:** Conduct surveys to understand the impact of sustainability initiatives on employee engagement and the perception of the company.

- **Analysis of environmental results:** Monitor specific environmental metrics, such as reduction in water and energy consumption, reduction of waste and increase in recycling rate.

- **Employee feedback:** Collect continuous feedback on sustainability programs to adjust and improve initiatives.

The adoption of sustainable practices reinforces the company's commitment to the future of the planet and promotes a feeling of purpose among employees. In the next chapter, **"THE ART OF LISTENING IN ENDOMARKETING"**, we will focus on the importance of actively listening to employees as a fundamental part of internal marketing strategies. The ability to listen and respond to employees' needs and feedback is essential to creating a positive and productive work environment, where everyone feels valued and an integral part of the company's success.

THE ART OF LISTENING IN ENDOMARKETING

The essence of effective internal marketing lies not only in communicating and engaging, but also in actively listening to employees. The art of listening is fundamental to understanding the team's needs, expectations and concerns, allowing the company to respond appropriately and build a work environment that reflects the values and objectives shared by everyone. This chapter addresses how to implement active listening strategies in the context of internal marketing to strengthen corporate culture and promote a more inclusive and productive environment.

THE IMPORTANCE OF ACTIVE LISTENING

Active listening in the corporate environment enables:

- **Identification of unexpressed needs:** Employees often have ideas or concerns that are not communicated through traditional channels. Active listening helps identify these issues.

- **Strengthening trust:** When employees realize that they are heard, trust in leadership and the organization increases.

- **Promotion of innovation:** Innovative ideas can emerge from any level of the organization. Actively listening to employees encourages creativity and innovation.

- **Improved engagement:** Employees who feel heard tend to engage more deeply with the company's objectives.

STRATEGIES TO PROMOTE ACTIVE LISTENING

To effectively incorporate active listening into internal marketing strategies:

- **Creating open communication channels:** Develop channels where employees can express their ideas, feedback and concerns anonymously or openly, such as suggestion boxes, discussion forums and regular surveys.

- **Implementation of regular feedback sessions:** Organize

periodic meetings dedicated to feedback, where employees can share their opinions and ideas directly with leadership.

- **Training for leaders and managers:** Offer active listening training for leaders and managers, emphasizing the importance of understanding and responding to the team's needs.

TRANSFORMING FEEDBACK INTO ACTION

Listening is just the first step; It is essential that the feedback received is transformed into concrete actions:

- **Analysis and response to feedback:** Regularly evaluate the feedback collected and develop action plans to address the issues raised.

- **Communication of changes:** Clearly communicate any changes or initiatives developed in response to employee feedback, reinforcing the idea that the company values and acts based on the team's opinions.

- **Monitoring results:** Monitor the results of implemented actions, using them to continually adjust internal marketing strategies.

Adopting active listening as an integral part of internal marketing creates a more transparent, inclusive and collaborative work environment, where all employees feel valued and an integral part of the company's success. In the next chapter, **"ENDOMARKETING AND THE EMPLOYEE EXPERIENCE"**, we will focus on how internal marketing strategies can be designed and implemented to improve the overall experience of employees in the company, covering everything from onboarding to continuous development, ensuring a work environment that not only retains talent, but makes them thrive.

ENDOMARKETING AND THE EMPLOYEE EXPERIENCE

Improving the employee experience is fundamental to retaining talent, increasing productivity and building a strong corporate culture. Internal marketing plays a crucial role in this process, offering tools and strategies to enrich each stage of the employee's journey within the company. This chapter explores how to use internal marketing to improve the employee experience, from the moment of onboarding to the development of a long and rewarding career.

UNDERSTANDING THE EMPLOYEE EXPERIENCE

The employee experience encompasses all touchpoints and interactions an employee has with the company, including:

- **Onboarding:** The initial introduction and integration process into the company.

- **Professional development:** Opportunities for growth and learning within the organization.

- **Work environment:** The everyday atmosphere, including company culture, physical space and available tools.

- **Recognition and reward:** How work and achievements are recognized and celebrated.

ENDOMARKETING STRATEGIES TO IMPROVE THE EXPERIENCE

To optimize the employee experience through internal marketing:

- **Creative onboarding programs:** Use internal marketing to create onboarding programs that not only inform, but also engage and inspire new employees, presenting the company's culture in an interactive way.

- **Continuous communication:** Keep communication channels always open and active, ensuring that employees are informed, involved and heard.

- **Development and training:** Promote professional

development opportunities through internal marketing campaigns that encourage participation in training, workshops and other forms of learning.

- **Recognition initiatives:** Create recognition programs that celebrate employees' achievements in a meaningful way, using internal marketing to highlight these moments.

CREATING A POSITIVE WORK ENVIRONMENT

The work environment is a key component of the employee experience. Effective strategies include:

- **Inclusive and inspiring workspaces:** Use internal marketing to promote the importance of a workspace that encourages creativity, collaboration and well-being.

- **Positive feedback culture:** Encourage a culture where feedback is seen as a tool for growth, highlighting stories of how feedback has led to personal and organizational improvements.

- **Events and activities:** Organize events and activities that reinforce the company culture and promote social interaction, contributing to a richer and more satisfying work experience.

MEASURING EFFECTIVENESS AND ADJUSTING STRATEGIES

To ensure that internal marketing initiatives are truly improving the employee experience:

- **Satisfaction and engagement surveys:** Carry out regular surveys to assess employees' perception of their experience at the company.

- **Feedback analysis:** Collect and analyze ongoing feedback on different aspects of the employee experience, using this information to adjust and improve initiatives.

- **Performance indicators:** Monitor key indicators, such as turnover rate, productivity and work quality, to evaluate the impact of internal marketing strategies on the employee experience.

Improving the employee experience through internal marketing is an ongoing process that requires attention to detail and a commitment to constant improvement. In the next chapter, **"INNOVATION AND CREATIVITY IN ENDOMARKETING**", we will explore how to encourage innovation and creativity within internal marketing strategies, ensuring that the company not only meets employees' current expectations, but also anticipates and adapts to future changes, maintaining Stay ahead in a competitive market.

INNOVATION AND CREATIVITY IN ENDOMARKETING

Innovation and creativity are crucial elements to keep internal marketing strategies dynamic, engaging and effective. By cultivating an environment that encourages innovation and values creativity, companies can not only improve the employee experience, but also foster a spirit of continuous evolution and adaptation. This chapter addresses how to integrate innovation and creativity into internal marketing initiatives, encouraging the active participation of employees and promoting a vibrant organizational culture.

FOSTERING A CREATIVE ENVIRONMENT

To encourage innovation and creativity in internal marketing, it is essential:

- **Promote freedom of expression:** Create a safe environment where employees feel free to share ideas, suggestions and feedback without fear of judgment.

- **Encourage divergent thinking:** Encourage employees to think "outside the box", considering new perspectives and unusual approaches to the company's challenges.

- **Offer resources and tools:** Provide the tools and resources necessary for employees to explore their creative ideas, such as design software, spaces for brainstorming and time dedicated to innovation.

CREATIVE STRATEGIES IN ACTION

Incorporating creativity into internal marketing campaigns can take several forms:

- **Innovative themed campaigns:** Develop internal marketing campaigns with creative and innovative themes that capture employees' attention and encourage participation.

- **Gamification:** Apply gamification elements in new and creative ways to engage employees, such as innovation competitions or sustainability challenges.

- **Stories and narratives:** Use storytelling to share successes, challenges and employees' journeys, creating an emotional connection and promoting the company's values.

ENCOURAGING EMPLOYEE PARTICIPATION

For innovation and creativity initiatives to be successful, it is vital to encourage the active participation of employees:

- **Creativity workshops:** Hold workshops that teach creativity and innovation techniques, encouraging employees to apply them in real projects.

- **Innovation spaces:** Create dedicated spaces where employees can work on innovative ideas, whether individually or as a team.

- **Recognition of innovative ideas:** Establish recognition programs for ideas and projects that contribute significantly to the company's objectives, valuing creative contributions.

MEASURING THE IMPACT OF CREATIVITY AND INNOVATION

Evaluate the success of creative and innovative initiatives through:

- **Direct feedback:** Collect feedback from employees on internal marketing initiatives, specifically asking about the most and least effective aspects in terms of encouraging creativity.

- **Participation analysis:** Monitor participation levels in proposed activities, identifying which strategies generate greater engagement.

- **Impact on the company's results:** Evaluate how the innovative ideas arising from these initiatives contributed to the improvement of the company's processes, products or services.

Injecting innovation and creativity into internal marketing strategies not only revitalizes engagement initiatives, but also contributes to a dynamic and adaptable corporate culture. In the next chapter, "**LEADERSHIP AND ENDOMARKETING**", we will explore the crucial role of leaders in promoting and supporting internal marketing initiatives, highlighting how effective leadership can amplify the results of these strategies and promote a positive and innovative work environment.

LEADERSHIP AND ENDOMARKETING

Leadership plays a fundamental role in the success of internal marketing initiatives. Effective leaders not only communicate the company's goals and values, but also act as ambassadors of organizational culture, inspiring and motivating their team to fully engage. This chapter addresses the importance of leadership in the context of internal marketing, offering strategies for leaders to promote a positive and innovative work environment.

THE ROLE OF LEADERS IN ENDOMARKETING

Effective leaders are essential for:

- **Model organizational culture:** Through their actions and decisions, leaders demonstrate the company's values, serving as models for employees to follow.

- **Communicate vision and goals:** Leaders clearly articulate the company's vision and goals, ensuring that all team members understand their role in organizational success.

- **Foster engagement:** Through recognition and support for professional development, leaders encourage active participation and commitment from employees.

STRATEGIES FOR LEADERS TO STRENGTHEN ENDOMARKETING

To maximize the positive impact of internal marketing leadership:

- **Development of communication skills:** Leaders must constantly improve their communication skills, ensuring that messages are transmitted effectively and empathetically.

- **Promotion of internal marketing initiatives:** Leaders must be at the forefront of internal marketing initiatives, actively participating and encouraging their team to do the same.

- **Creating spaces for feedback:** Establish channels for two-way feedback, where employees feel free to express ideas, concerns and suggestions.

- **Public recognition:** Adopt public recognition practices, valuing employees' contributions and reinforcing the importance of each individual to the company's success.

OVERCOMING LEADERSHIP CHALLENGES

Some challenges leaders may face include:

- **Resistance to change:** Leaders can work to overcome resistance, demonstrating the benefits of internal marketing initiatives and involving the team in the change process.

- **Maintain authenticity:** Leaders must strive to maintain authenticity, ensuring that actions and communications genuinely reflect the company's values and culture.

- **Adaptation to the needs of the team:** Recognize and adapt to the diverse needs of the team, promoting an inclusive and supportive environment.

LEADERSHIP IN ACTION: SUCCESS STORIES

Stories of leaders who positively impacted their teams through effective internal marketing strategies can serve as inspiration. Whether through innovative recognition campaigns or leading by example in sustainability initiatives, these cases highlight how leadership can amplify the results of internal marketing strategies and promote an engaged and motivated corporate culture.

Leadership is an essential component in internal marketing, acting as a catalyst for employee engagement and motivation. In the next chapter, **"BUILDING AN ENDOMARKETING TEAM"**, we will explore how to build a dedicated team within the company to lead and execute internal marketing strategies, ensuring that initiatives are consistent, innovative and aligned with organizational goals.

BUILDING AN ENDOMARKETING TEAM

For internal marketing strategies to be successful and sustainable in the long term, it is crucial to form a dedicated team that can lead and execute these initiatives within the company. An effective internal marketing team serves as the heart of internal communications operations, ensuring that messages are consistent, innovative and aligned with organizational culture and objectives. This chapter focuses on building and strengthening this team, highlighting the necessary skills, responsibilities, and best practices to maximize your impact.

DEFINING THE ROLE OF THE ENDOMARKETING TEAM

The internal marketing team is responsible for:

- **Develop internal communication strategies:** Create and implement plans that promote company culture, engage employees and improve the work experience.

- **Coordinate internal marketing campaigns:** Manage campaigns that align employees with the company's objectives, using creative and innovative tools.

- **Monitor and evaluate results:** Measure the effectiveness of internal marketing strategies, adjusting them as necessary to meet organizational objectives.

BUILDING AN EFFECTIVE TEAM

To build a robust internal marketing team, consider:

- **Skills diversity:** Include members with a wide range of skills, from communications and graphic design to data analysis and organizational psychology.

- **Cultural alignment:** Choose employees who deeply understand and are aligned with the company culture, as this will facilitate authentic and effective communication.

- **Capacity for innovation:** Look for individuals with a propensity for creativity and innovation, essential to keeping internal marketing strategies dynamic and engaging.

BEST PRACTICES FOR LEADING AN ENDOMARKETING TEAM

- **Establish clear objectives:** Set specific and measurable goals for the team, ensuring that everyone is aligned with the organization's larger goals.

- **Promote collaboration:** Encourage collaboration not only within the team, but also with other departments, to ensure that internal marketing initiatives are integrated into the company's overall strategies.

- **Invest in professional development:** Provide training and development opportunities for team members, helping them improve their skills and stay up to date with the latest trends in internal communications and internal marketing.

- **Celebrate successes:** Recognize and celebrate team successes, reinforcing the positive impact of their contributions to the company.

COMMON CHALLENGES AND HOW TO OVERCOME THEM

Building and maintaining an effective internal marketing team can present challenges, including:

- **Budget restrictions:** Look for creative, low-cost solutions for internal marketing initiatives, maximizing available resources.

- **Internal resistance:** Work to gain the support of leaders and employees, demonstrating the value of internal marketing strategies for the company's general objectives.

- **Maintaining team engagement:** Keep the team motivated and engaged by providing regular positive feedback and opportunities for personal and professional growth.

An effective internal marketing team is vital for developing and implementing strategies that strengthen corporate culture and improve employee engagement. In the next chapter, **"TRANSFORMING THEORY INTO ACTION"**, we will summarize the concepts discussed previously, highlighting the importance of putting internal marketing strategies into practice to transform unmotivated employees into an engaged and dedicated workforce, and create a positive and productive work environment. productive.

TRANSFORMING THEORY INTO ACTION

Throughout this book, we explore the wide range of strategies and practices that make up the universe of internal marketing. From the importance of understanding demotivation in the workplace to creating a team dedicated to internal marketing, to integrating sustainability and innovation into internal initiatives, each chapter provided valuable insights to transform theory into action. This concluding chapter highlights the importance of implementing the internal marketing strategies discussed, with the aim of converting unmotivated employees into an engaged and dedicated team, and creating a positive and productive work environment.

THE IMPORTANCE OF ACTING

Theory, however complete and inspiring it may be, only has value when transformed into concrete action. Each internal marketing strategy discussed in this book has the potential to significantly transform your company's culture, but this potential can only be realized through practical implementation and an ongoing commitment to improving and adapting internal practices.

STEPS TO IMPLEMENTATION

- **Assess your company's needs:** Start with an honest assessment of your organization's specific needs and challenges. Identify areas for improvement in engagement and internal communication.

- **Develop a strategic plan:** Based on the initial assessment, develop a strategic internal marketing plan that addresses the identified areas. Set clear and measurable objectives.

- **Mobilize your team:** Engage leaders and employees in the process, explaining the benefits of internal marketing and how it can improve the work environment for everyone.

- **Execute with excellence:** Implement planned initiatives with attention to detail, ensuring that each action is well communicated and executed.

- **Measure and adjust:** Use established metrics to evaluate the success of your internal marketing strategies. Be open to feedback and ready to make adjustments as needed.

MAINTAINING LONG-TERM COMMITMENT

Internal marketing is not a quick fix, but rather an ongoing commitment to developing a strong corporate culture and an engaged workforce. This requires:

- **Flexibility and adaptation:** Be prepared to adapt your strategies as the company and the work environment evolve.

- **Continuous investment:** Recognize internal marketing as an essential investment in the well-being of your employees and the success of your company.

- **Culture of continuous improvement:** Foster a culture that values feedback and is always looking for ways to improve.

LOOKING TO THE FUTURE

By turning internal marketing theory into action, you not only improve the current work environment, but also lay the foundation for a brighter and more productive future for your company. We encourage you to stay focused on your internal marketing goals, celebrate your achievements and learn from challenges along the way.

This book provided the map, but the journey is yours. As you embark on this journey of transformation, remember that internal marketing success depends not only on the strategies you implement, but more importantly, on the passion, creativity and commitment you and your team bring to these initiatives every day. . Move forward with courage, creativity and conviction, turning theory into action and, ultimately, action into lasting success.

As we turn the final page of this journey together, I sincerely hope that the learnings shared here have touched your heart and sparked new perspectives. If this book has brought you any value, I kindly ask that you take a few moments to leave a review on Amazon. Your words not only help me grow and hone my craft, but they also guide other readers in their quests for knowledge and inspiration. Your opinion is a valuable gift, both for me and for the community of readers looking for stories that transform. I sincerely thank you for sharing this journey with me and I hope we can meet again in the pages of a new adventure.

REGINALDO OSNILDO

Hello, I'm Reginaldo Osnildo, author and innovator in the fields of sales, technology, and communication strategies. My background spans from the academic setting, as a professor and researcher at the University of Southern Santa Catarina, to hands-on strategy development at the Catarinense Radio Group. With a PhD in sales narratives and digital convergence, and a Master's in storytelling and social imaginary, I offer my readers a unique blend of theory and practice. My aim is to deliver knowledge in a simple, practical, and didactic language, encouraging direct application in one's personal and professional life.

Yours sincerely

Reginaldo Osnildo

+55 48 991913865

reginaldoosnildo@gmail.com

www.ingramcontent.com/pod-product-compliance
Lightning Source LLC
Chambersburg PA
CBHW050326230526
45471CB00005B/2365